# salmonpoetry

*Publishing Irish & International
Poetry Since 1981*

the arts council
an chomhairle ealaíon

funding
literature

artscouncil.ie

# Jo Slade

## Cycles and Lost Monkeys

Published in 2019 by
Salmon Poetry
Cliffs of Moher, County Clare, Ireland
Website: www.salmonpoetry.com
Email: info@salmonpoetry.com

ISBN 978-1-912561-66-7

Cover & Title Page Image:
*Queue* by Jo Slade

Cover Design & Typesetting: *Siobhán Hutson*

*Printed in Ireland by Sprint Print*

*Salmon Poetry gratefully acknowledges the support of*
*The Arts Council / An Chomhairle Ealaíon*

*"As if poems were the earth's dreams."*

Raúl Zurita

# Contents

# Cycles and Lost Monkeys

We're cycling through woods
in tandem
singing songs from childhood
We're cycling home –
if we can find it?

*"Roll along covered wagon, roll along…"*

We're children in our heads
with the same fear –
"Only one?" someone asks
A voice from the back shouts
"Abandonment-baby"
Then a swaying melody
and the song –

*"to the turn of your wheels I'll sing a song"*

One calls out loudly
"Move on"

Memory is a derelict cinema
with red velvet seats and a hole in the wall
where an eye festers

"Move on"

The first house we pass is made of stone

Is this where I belong?

I drop my bike to the ground
and rush over

the doors are boarded with planks
the windows blackened with paint

My companions are impatient —
we're older
time is imperative

"Move along"

We're cycling through a painting by de Balincourt
a man waves in the distance
calls us deeper through trees

"There it is!"

The painter's tree is tall and golden
I want to climb to the top
to a wavering house
climb and climb never stop

We're going through a forest of faces
blink-eyes like stars
hang from branches

The second house is obscured
we almost speed past it
I peddle up to the window
and lean into the dark —
six steel beds suspend from a beam
and six winter jackets
a mothers' toile evening gown
and a christening garment —

an heirloom for a baby
who didn't want to grow
so she cut off the sleeves
to make it her own

Then a choir of voices
suffuse the darkness

The song ends.

My companions are gone

their bicycles are piled in the forest
like skeletons – a genocide of wheels
and chains

A band of noise rattles on
through the century –
fathers return with scarred faces

some die where they fall
others die in cells
like placentas

Sunlight bites branches
bullets spark off the spokes
as I hum

*"to the song we were singing, roll along"*

I cycle on alone
A house peeps through hedges:
its windows are shattered
glass is scattered in shards
leaves on trees are diamonds of blood
lit by a flickering torch

A home in the woods
with birds and ghosts
and a surveillance monitor?

Faces blur on the screen
one is clear: a baby's face
covered in hair
or is it fur?

One is better than none
if it sees
if it hasn't stopped listening

# I see them in the distance

sliding by on a conveyor of souls

She is there

always with a willing smile

that draws light from me

light that fills the middle distance

so space becomes an ocean of waves

gently pushing the shore

What world am I locked into

my skull dark with imaginings?

I see them I can feel their warmth

as though they were the living

and I have died in a century of images

# Boat

The desperate who sail

in a nightmare know

the boat is a promise

they call out in darkness

they want to be born

so they can be saved

# a small child mouths words

an inner music fills her

she tip-taps her shoes

hears inside her bone secret

# Raqqa

Children are in the street chanting
in unison they lift their rifles
like javelins into the future
Innocent of pride and power
they're an open pasture
the master has come to inhabit

The elders have nothing to say
even to speak
is against the rule of life

# After such a fall

In a house not far from here
in a shoebox under a bed
a heart beats in pink tissue paper
She dreads the nights    where they take her
wrapped in black so the moon
can't save her
through a hole in the bed
down a tunnel she topples
over and over
into a pool as deep and cool
as a sailor's palm    as round as a penny
if you see her    catch her
and bring her home
her body drenched her jimmies torn
She'll slip like a lip through a vacant lot
if you don't stop her
She'll disappear
or reappear in a deadly spot
She never cries
she lies stiff as steel
inside a dream she can't remember
Oh tell her not to dwell there
tell her not to dwell there

# Someone

close by is sawing wood

they're putting up a barricade

in their common garden

The sun won't loose

its metallic smile on a neighbour

old smell of pewter in a corner

and yet

the bright spode sky is here

and a bird sings

a tree lists like a ladder

against the day

sore to the sound of timber

# Assassin

is in his palace of faces

Night calms itself

steels itself like a stubborn child

There's a bird warbling in a tree

its pearl eye can be seen

like a moon through leaves

I sit in my hut and listen

I see known faces from every angle

shine like rain on windows

I grieve

Someone paces the turret

silent as a shadow

His gun raised

His bird coming into view

# I turn my back on the world

and a tidal-bat of ignominy cracks off me

Mercy drags me away – sometimes

it almost kills me

I let my back take the whack

wave after wave of war

abysmal days common tortures:

women's fist-marked faces

boy-soldiers with guns –

when they open their mouths

their futures explode

Cover the stranger in a cloak a raincoat

a hoodie – hide her among ruins in Homs

let her sleep beneath her city

Oh where is the white tree

the one that grows out of pity?

# Dolls

She loves her paper dolls
their clip on clothes
their sumptuous mouths
their eyes that never close
their silence.
She loves the feel of fingers
inside scissor holes
the sharpness of the shapes
how they emerge
cut-out corpses in designer clothes.
At night she dreams them real
they scare her in their layers:
furs and silks plaids and pearls.
She hears them whisper secrets
in their paper world
and snicker –
she hates them then
their arrogance and filthy tongues
She'd tear them limb from limb
if she could –
she'd cut their hair
black their eyes
she'd put them back inside the book
and listen to their cries.

# Power

has a face ornate as a cathedral

benign as white dust as crystal

His voice says *there's nothing to fear*

Then an explosion next-door or distant?

Children pick through the debris

blinded by dust and cruelty

# I'm writing a way through winter

my snow-filled pen a sprawl

of linear hoarfrost

a calligraphy loosely formed

on a window —

the heart's flame like winter sun

rising in the east

severe at that moment

if you're out there in the white field

# Zero

I'm in Iceland on the coldest day, among a gang of hippies and caribou.
I have a sleigh. I just spotted an Arctic tern and the shadow of wings
like something fleeting she said to me.
I thought of the word vision and of her crossing the frozen grass
in a park somewhere near a coast. There she is, sitting in a cinema chair
snow settling on her hair and she's wearing her fur collar.
She's warm, lost in the lives that flit by on the screen.
I'm writing on the tissue inside my skull. I'm keeping count of caribou
and days, of the number of stars that appear on the surface of a pot of ice.
Soon, we'll make the great sled journey across the snow plains to that other life.


*for Fanny*

# Underground

The station emptied and filled
it was light then it grew dark

I stood for days on the same spot
I slept on my feet
I was waiting for a carriage of children

A voice overheard asked the question:
"Is this Liverpool Street station
is this my destination?"

A train appeared out of a dark tunnel
crowded with adults
and their stifling fears

Commuters pushed forward
as if in a dream
they flung books at doors
that wouldn't open
glazed eyes stared back at them

I stepped onto the tracks
I wandered the tunnels
to find a way out

A torch blazed a hole in the earth
I climbed up and like a seed
drifted into the world

# There's a lie curled beneath the baby

when the moon enters her room
it swallows her —

but the lie pulls her back
by her pudgy toes

As the baby grows
she's brave enough to slay
the moon's sham of silver

# Ghosts

My house is home to ghosts
they enter through cracks

they come with specks of blood
on their palms ash on their feet

they have come a long way
they never sleep

they move from room to room
without a sound

one searches for a nest of eggs
one's mouth is open to eat

another carries his brother:
a baby with a bomb in his fleece


there is the sigh of the wind
and the tree that speaks to the dark


and the flat immovable land
and heat from a burnt-out heart


They have nowhere to go
everything complicit – incredulous

The dream was vivid:
children from a frontier town

corralled by a rabid dog


Let them feel the wind that will take
them away – let them see the house

with the white scarf
the blind eye inside the window

# Palimpsest

Floating beneath us     inside the crystal palace     their names
are dead to our ears

Their names     silent in the pitiless deep appear
like ghosts at our feet

The lines stretch on forever     beads of water forming a chain
ascending and descending into the waves

Do not walk on their names do not disturb the dust of their bones

Only the birds weightless as air are borne upward by their names
only then the forgotten people

flesh of their bodies blood in their veins

and the birds yearning for them     their song fading out (as we stand here)
mesmerized     by their names     dissolving

(as when they lay there) on a beach somewhere in the Mediterranean

their remains sinking into the sand that is always moving
clearing the foreshore of debris

the sea drawing away     waves washing over our shame

# sign

a sign:

gold and brown

the leaf

that lies hidden

in the ground

# Figs

A man wakes in another room, in another bed. Nothing is as it was.
Later, he will come to know time intimately. Outside sun shines –
day waits for him to arrive. His carer, compelled by kindness
lifts him from bed to chair to an opened window.
He feels the winter chill and sees, though his sight is impaired
children playing in the square. The room becomes clammy
the atmosphere grows heavy with over-ripeness, like rotting fruit.
This is how it is growing old, prowling the perimeters of youth
watching through an hourglass apples perish in the cold.
The mind wishes for peace, it lays down with time
it extracts juice of compassion from the sweetness of figs.

# Auteville

The shape of you in the window
your back framed by its dark lines.
Brightness beyond and sounds
that meld into the distance.
Your skeleton appears through your skin
as you lean out – strain to see something
I can't see – something visible to you
in which you are wholly present.

I lie back & trace the outline of your body
finger trembling ...
your eyes elsewhere, over everything:
the garden, the houses, the lush fields
like wings leaving the mountain.

*for Richard*

# Bell

Inside the old woman a boat chugs on a still lake. All her life
the promise of travel. Trails of thought linger, like the aroma
of jasmine and colours she imagines of Africa and India.
This time she travels alone. She leaves all she owns: her children
her home, even her name is ether. She has a self inside herself
who looks out, into a distance of rivers and trees. She is the same
as an infant, unnamed by presence. It is early morning the world is silent.
The old woman boards a ferry, she tucks her bag beside her
she holds tight to the rails. The boat rocks on a rhythmic current
but she doesn't think about danger, if she did she wouldn't move.
She trusts herself to the self inside her. In her hand is a small
brass bell with raised images of elephants, trunks to tails
in an endless circle. The old woman hears the mynah bird sing
and tastes the perfume of pine on her tongue, sprays of water cover her.
Perhaps I will find her, she thinks.

# Precipice

I have held on for so long

to a ribbon of faith

between me and the cliff face

it stretches —

attached to nothing

# Hive

She wished for sweetness –
a common cure for heart's hurt,
where there was sadness
now there'd be no more.
So, he bought her honey
in pots the shape of breasts –
as round a curve
would hold life's liquid, gold.
He put them on a shelf –
they glittered, glistened
the pots reflected a convex image
where edges blurred and pain dissolved.
A kind of axis turned the honeyed eye
she saw him inside the hive –
his wings winnowing the perfumed air.

*for Richard*

It will be her second winter coming next, the broken woman I found in a skip and saved her. Saved her who fell or slept and forgot to wake — small statuette I fixed her broken legs, her severed breasts I replaced with cups I put a stick in the hollow of her wrist, to hang a lamp, at night she has a purpose: my guide to hiddenness stands, between the fig tree and the rose no taller than my arm, at arm's length the span to touch her flame when it is lit — along a rail of light she breathes her livingness.

# Fables

Each time the baby leapt in her belly the string broke and she'd tie it again.
She was reminded of a girl she'd seen, how she turned a length of string
round and around her fingers, making a complex puzzle.


Each time the monk hit the wood, the sound of his axe echoed
inside the walls of the monastery. In his pocket, in a jam jar, he kept a bee –
he was reminded how easy it is to enter the forest and find honey.


Each time the shopkeeper swept out his shop mice scurried beneath the boards.
He could hear them, but he couldn't catch them. He remembered how long
it takes a man to mine gold, how he can spend a whole life panning, for nothing.


Each time the hairdresser wrapped a head in a towel, the skin darkened
the eyes flashed like two coals. She saw her sister in the mirror
and heard her whisper huddled in a corner of a souk.
She remembered the distance she'd travelled, how glass holds a truth.


Each time a storm enters the lighthouse, bones of the dead appear on the cliff.
The keeper carves them into fish that swim in the deep. Out in the ocean oars
are eternally rowing. The keeper is silent. He remembers the last wind that struck
how a boat of migrants broke off the rock and no one but death to find them.

# Script

Words flew into my heart
from a nearby house
We were thinking the same thought:
about love in the Soviet


A bird fluttered on the periphery
a secondary character
in a play of shadows


A man shouted into my face
another wore class like a grace
he shared everything


In the presence of grotesque belief
the spirit curls at my feet
like a child in a boat
at sea off the coast


I'm reading from a new script
words that will sound
in a cool anterior

# O lavender hands

the stained pavement

the purple road

Most beautiful of days

and these ravines:

trails of violet and pink

# Tarot

A black and white photograph lay on the table: a heavy man posed
as a monument, his bearded chin rested on a large, fisted hand.
He was upside down the way monuments often appear in dreams
or as major arcana in a tarot reading. It always means bad news
or at least the reverse of free-thinking. Monuments are man's things
like handcuffs or cuff links. Stone effigies raised high,
so their heads interrupt infinity. A tare in the photograph implied
carelessness, as if he'd been buried alive, forgotten
inside a shoebox of memorabilia. From his imposing head came
the sweetest sound – I was reminded of something my mother said
about an obese opera singer, "there's a small bird in his throat"
and there was, because when the singer died a bird flew
from his mouth shedding feathers of soft, blue light.

# On Reflective Memory:
# I Wish I had Been Wiser

The heart is its own master
It opens without guile to all it sees
It believes because it feels


The sound of a drum     far off
in the hills where we once lived


The house is the same
nothing has changed
and the river that flows through it
and the forest of shadows
we stumbled into


What I remember:
a hood pulled over my head
eyes downcast
the body's fear of annihilation


The paradox of care:
holding another's heart
knowing that if the earth quakes
we lose everything


That sorrow rises
its lament like a bird returning
to the same nest
on the threshold of darkness

Time and memory – the body and its days
Who were they the young women
mesmerized
thought erased by anticipation?


The woman-child sharp eyed
from a corner
The world spinning
the woman dizzy with speed
the child clinging on
lest she spiral downward


They opened us   petal by petal
to find the wound
They dressed it with a litany of words:
wood-leaf  lint  mecuricome  cloves


Nothing was as it seemed
We are here    Now
evidence lies in the sacred space
between our eyes


In a foreign city we walk in parks
you count the trees
We have made the most of our lives:
the views the promises
the quiet squares we return to

No right word
nor perfectly drawn line
but to feel protected
to not feel shame   is divine


Ships come and go to the city —
someone inured to sleep
watches waves turn to ripples of light
In the harbour a tree grows
that sees beyond the horizon
to a more wondrous place
Saramago    is there
a more wondrous place?


*for Pauline*

# Shelter

I hear Freddy King sing, H*elp me Through the Day Help me Through the Night*
and I shimmy through the door shoulders rising, body swaying.
I'm holding a hairbrush, miming his words.

It's August, the 70s and he's singing,
*"your sweet loving will make everything alright."*

Sound and mime, the pang and sigh of being young,
alone, headphones on, singing in a darkened room with Jagger,
                    *"Gimme, gimme shelter"*
air guitar throbbing, the ping and slip of fingers fret the heart-chords
hold their measure...

Whenever I'm scared and I was then,
I'd whisper my inner blues.

Twilight – shade falling, the shadow of someone passing the door?
The other side will open someday – where we are, will be there.
Who felt the undulating rhythm: the birds, the cat pulling knot balls of hair
or the one sitting at an upstairs window, reading the weather?

I sing out the high notes, sing to hear myself, Here, Here...
and 'I' is you looking back and forward, a two faced Janus
not clear about the questions, no answers but a tune we could hum
and humming feel its route through the body, like a river.

A bird perched on the garage roof its throaty call, a sound
I've come to know: the nearness and the distance
an emptying cry, like a wilderness I'd wandered into.


Sister of the 60s my slight and eager soul –
voices, like Etta James or Joni unfurling, enfolding, curling
their tongues to warm my bones.


Sunlight, a wisp of gold glimmers, reveals husks of unforgiving life.
There is no going back.


We're here, one with cloud and rain, washed over, momentarily glorious.

# Berlin

       morning     sky ochre and pink
I'm waking in the east side of the city
solemn blocks of grey stretch high and wide
trees interrupt the sterility.
What part of me carries this sky
hears a bell-like memory
and is swept into the open space
among autumn trees
and these austere buildings?

Everyday I wake the city is within:
its sky its trees the buildings.
A blue sound in the river and humming
as of an old man returning –
someone I have yet to meet?

A red line stains the horizon
as if the city were burning.
Sorrow breaths a long breath
the page inks    draws a solitary grief
and I am between two cities
and there is no difference
There is no difference.

# I walked into the sea into
# an ocean of crystal

and swam with the sun.
I dived beneath the surface
that shattered and split.
I knew I had entered the unknown.

The cold was so intense fish froze and lay
in layers on the sea bed.
I swam through them —
they were like stars twinkling overhead
and the deep became flooded with moonlight.

I wished I'd swam back to the world
I'd come from with its derelict houses
its overgrown gardens and lay in grass
staring up at the trees and watched shadows
brush over branches —
even this would have pleased me.

To be back there as skies darkened or lightened
and the world became covered
in snow frozen and silent.

# Then when the forest was red and golden

and white trees stood like sentinels
in the cold air
and the earth beneath rippled
with other life
eager and inevitable — I stood there

and felt time open around me
and the long distances close
and for an instant I thought
of my own insignificance

how I would lose everything
and my breath so precious now
would rise
a faint glow into the night sky

and I would hear the sounds
of the universe
and know the deep silence
into which I will go.

# Trace

Organ sounds drift the air    mellow the stillness    not into actuality

but a transcendent other space

Echoes hover in the shadows    in the cool of this small chapel

in Villefranc des Largais


I'm pacing the cobbled nave    beseeching the stone faces

to hear my anxiety

but the mute ones in their arched niches stare passed me

into the distance    a fixed vision I'm not part of

though I want to    see

I stretch my hand over the flame    touch the stone eye

trace the line disappearing    outward    beyond my imagining

through walls    into the open

away from this seeing place    this silence    split

by someone in a dark balcony playing a requiem for the unseen

# Awning

Toward the end of his life he sat under an awning, sun warmed his feet.
He tilted his old head back. Something, he thought, would assuage his grief –
if not the sun, then the shadow cast by the awning, or an image would appear
from childhood: his mother's face, or a broken statue of the little flower,
arm full of roses. The reality of grief would be interrupted. Sleep would happen
and  dreams and he'd wake back at the place before grief.
His father appeared out of a mist, not as he expected, not as  he used to be,
pale and tormented. A more youthful man stood before him, excited by a prospect?
They sat talking and he remembered his father's violent eruptions,
how they overtook him and the fear he felt, the child fleeing again into the fairy wood.
He saw his father wince, he heard him weep, but it was too late.
Momentarily grief suspended, like a leaf caught in a web.

# By its secret sign

the soul invites

daylight

the taste of yellow on a green stem

a bowl of pomegranates in a room

the smell of rose madder

# Solipsist

And so, (as in the continuation of all stories…) she awoke with courage.
Resolute, she prepared for the outing, excited for the first time
this end of her life. The minibus drew up outside her apartment.
She looked down at the quiet street, at the stark trees that reached
their bare arms up and noticed a small child coaxing a wheel with a stick.
For a second she thought it was her friend Marcel, as she remembered him
in a blue and white sailor's suit. This is the imposition of memory
when we step back into an imagined past. I say imagined, since so much
occurred between them. She knows this, but the taste, the smell, the comfort
of friendship is still there, a presence she can feel immersed in –
Marcel's heavy-lidded eyes, like dark wells, secluded, even frightening.
Then a swan flew over the child's head and the minibus backed slowly
toward the entrance, making little beeps as safety steps were released.
She climbed in and sat at a window. She held her own hands like strangers
as if Marcel and she were being formally introduced. Always close, they often
talked and kissed. Memory became the movement that propelled her.
What she sees: the trees, the child, the swan are passed, even her flesh
has become strange. All that remains is the minibus that carries
her forward and the belief, that only her own mind exists.

# Metamorphosis

*after Titian*

Last tendrils of the rose spread and bloom

everything comes forward    grows    as I approach

(from the back of the crowd) the painting

with its incredible blue and its perfect bodies

that unlike a rose are ageless.

An area of overwhelming bleakness hides

in the right-hand corner of the canvas –

I move closer and can smell mud, a damp odour.


Edges are familiar: dark places sun never reaches

the thick glutinous clay    same clay we're made of

same seed forming its own eye like a moon.


A glint of light enters    a blur of sun floods the canvas:

the leaves    the stream    the flesh…

whatever is at the centre    we know nothing of it.

# Mirror

*"one's a'self encounter"*

Emily Dickinson

When I look into the mirror I see myself
looking past my eyes toward a vacant space
that could be death or the anti-room to life?
I'm on a threshold if I enter the glass
I'll pass into another world.

Will I know myself – the shape I left a silhouette?
Will I see my death and grieve
will the self behind the self reveal?

# Blindness

As if a hand were cleaning my eye: a wiper of tender finger
moves back and forth, blurring and clearing. The sky is too bright.
Momentary blindness means I'm in an unknown space.
I experience great peace. Like a backstroke swimmer I feel my body
held up by water, whatever weighted me flows into the deep.
I believe I have come to an end, or I'm stuck in a beginning.
Silence inhabits me. A man on the beach peels into a fish suit
he too wants to lose himself, as if his life here were complete.
I hear him sigh from far away, like an old wind. A shape,
that must be light refracted, shines in the sky. Memories come and go.
A celestial body that could be my own, or the man's, drifts past me.
Sea anemones flash like hope in the long dark, or lights of a city
yet to be unearthed, or something I had known and forgotten:
a philosophy, a way of being that would reveal everything. As if
darkness would waken an awareness and water clear my vision.

# The wall

is a seam of grief

it divides the land

it runs through villages and schools

it sneaks into homes like a thief.


How can we speak of loss and promise

the harvest of bitter and sweet?

# Visitation

How far you have come, how deep you were down among bones
capillaries of air spilling into your mouth, making you breathe
and the smell of dank earth and the dark of which you've grown tired.
What crises of absence brings you back in your awakening dress
your meadow of hair, your fine fingers a tangle of vines?
Were you hoping to find yourself, unborn?
Are you wondering where the larch-bed you were laid in has gone
and why you're here in your green chair in a corner of my dream?
There was something I wanted to say to you, about sweeping
the leaves and hyacinths in the garden, about a photograph I found
of you and your first love, you're sitting on his knees, laughing –
you don't see war-clouds gathering, or the ash that clings to his lashes.
Your image fades, as the dream fades, lost in a haze of wakefulness.

# petals

like snow blown

and her sweeping them

bagging them

lest this be his last summer


*i.m Macdara Woods*

# Tree

Tall eucalyptus tree bends in the wind, how the green of its limbs
has faded, as if it had sprung from a forgotten day or something fell
from a great distance, through cloud and out through a haze turned
its frame pale and curved, as though with a nudge it would fall
and be easily broken. Wind ruffles its leaves like an old garment
moths fly from, still breath comes from the deep, through earth,
into its bark. The wind shifts to the east, a strange gust updrafting
and I'm watching the tree and its leaves quiver.
I hear children screech and further away someone laughing,
sounds that echo in the void like words that have ceased
or is it the moan of the wind as it stirs the high branches?
At evening the moon cloaks the tree in silver
like a child drooping in a fairy dress. The silence is comforting.
Somehow the word that was the tree has vanished.

i.m.

*for Tim*

# Light

Tim is on a bus travelling through frost and snow, perhaps in a wrong direction?
He didn't want to go, he wanted to stay and cook dinner for his family
and light the stove and sit and listen to their stories. In the cold people behave
as if night were a criminal: no good can come of it – but he's fearless
he knows silence is confusing and that rivers flow deep beneath the surface.
Frozen rain flies at the bus window and at trees huddled like children
along the road. When he arrives as he said he would, at that other destination
will he know in the dark which way to go? Will they show him the photograph:
the one where he's smiling, surrounded by familial faces?
When the light comes, what will he do with it?

# Your mouth opens

your head leans forward in sleep
Now a hand appears
like a moist leaf to feed you

Twilight on summers' street
the lost boy with his ball

You open your mouth
as if to speak

The last descent falls
on an urban estate.

# Compass

Let it all go, was my intuition. Some situations require
rational thinking: he was here, now he's gone.
My sister rang from far away, what she tried to say sounded urgent.
She was travelling alone, in Buenos Aires the night she phoned.
Stars filled the sky, exquisite night bowed above me. Her voice
rose and fell, words became tiny tremors – her sound was interrupted
by signals: codes, letters, numbers, something was using our distance
to transmit indescribable longing. I heard the word brother, or was it
other, or mother? I'd catch hisses, a pulse pounding, murmurs,
silence… then a howl like a wolf hurting, or a Madres in the Plaza de Mayo
and I thought of our brother how he disappeared one midsummer evening
and how we've been searching. A moment of closeness. I asked her:
are you in the square with them – with the grandmothers whose white scarves
billow like souls, are you waiting for him to return, a swallow buried in cloud?

# In my dream

birds

dropped

from the sky
their breasts still warm

My brother

who had recently died

fell

with them
(his dark eyes and usual smile)

This morning he stood at my kitchen window

I could see through him
like a ghost in a 60s movie

We were children

locked in the same vision.

# I stood at the window

and watched trains disappear

into darkness

The glass rattled

a streak of light flashed

a veil of melancholy covered the city


I do as my oculist advised

and keep binoculars on the sill


Will I recognize his shape

so like others at this distance

or his face

suddenly visible in the orange light

of a pedestrian crossing?

The White Cottage

# The White Cottage

the long road through the forest at Birkenau

the beautiful trees

leaves of the dead strewn on a path through the wood

the white cottage stood at the edge of a meadow

they walked there together     disrobed

entered the black door holding each other

# Birkenau

Be among us is what I hear them say

They want me to lie down in the grass

to listen    when earth speaks up to me

So I lie on that exact spot

and time draws my shape on the earth

a shape that is me    but not

not my breath    nor my heart beating fast

No    it is not time

though I am willing to look into their dark

though I laid down in the damp loam

and felt at home among their bones

# Sisters

Sisters    did you hear the sound of a train
at your shoulder?
*"It sped away through a tunnel of trees"*

Sisters    did you see crystals of snow
form to glaciers?
*"There were bodies in layers like thieves"*

Sisters    did you speak to your keepers?
*"They ransacked our quarters
language hid in a bunk with fleas"*

# 0

Nothing     has a voice
barks day and night
till the head hounds you

Nothing     breaths
it fills a length of passage like a sleeve

Nothing     pelts the beast
that lays in wait
numbers souls as ants
builds a chamber smokes them out

Nothing     sneaks the hut
can't quench its thirst
eyes some-one last never first
(Name Date Death)

Nothing     sleeps an instant on a blank
wipes the slate
will smudge the facts

Nothing has a human face
Stands around
Waits

# am

am hoisted am the shorn

am skin burned am numb

am unbound badly bruised

am steel in hand

am amenable am true

am moon-eyed am calm

am strangeness am wild

am ill-conceived

am child of darkness

and of light

am blood on your hands

in your mouth

am ice

# Chaff

Chaff winnowing the dead
spreads like wings
high above the sheds —
like moths worrying the light
that it might turn to flame
and burn them to ash again.

moonlight shimmies
the snow-field

a bell rings

stirs the sleeping moths

Inside the book of thought

winter

# Ghost Moth

Lamp-light drops into a blue pool

A moth rises in a swoop and flies

to the one spot it knows


Wind swept the earth

turned everything up

The sky     alien at first

filled with dust

moths adrift in the dark


Things fall apart: a house

on a hill with a cross

whole countries lost

How will we know them

the named

the eyes that dwell

where they flamed?

Night-gusts…

ghost moths throng this small space

wing-beats release a scent so potent

she comes

without tongue or mouth

The exactness of their fit and lift

Their fall

a long way down in darkness



The moth in its small world is master

In the stratosphere where the winged drift

everything is nothing and the same



In the deep they drift

silent as moons

What do they do in the dark

tinker the word chime

in the silence of heart?

# The Book

The Book that Hasn't Found me   The Book I'll Never Find   The Book Without Words   The Book of Abandoned Words   The Book of Children and Their Sounds   The Book That Turns its Pages and Sings its Story at Night Alone in the Dark   The Book of Transcendence or the shimmering surface The Book with No Beginning   The Book that Lives Inside Me   The Sleeping Book   The Book of Memory is Most Precious   The Book of Lost Things Glorious Bodies a book of organic matter   A Book of Painted Thoughts   Two Books of Love Undying   A Book of Self-Love   The Child Eugenia subtitled A Life on Fire   The Book of Snow   The Book of Ways one direction Ornithology's Book of Fine Feathers   Book of the North   Book of Flies Book of Tears   The Book of Innards what you dare not see   The Book of Dissolution   The Book of Names   The Big Book of Births   The Book of Landscape description is the art in writing   The Book of the Sublime and the Desublimed   Book of Sexual Fantasies   The Book of Terror: I found terror of darkness and the unbound   A Book of Masks subtitled future faces   The Book of Instincts also called no place for reason   The Book of Light in Language   The Book of Privation   The Small Book of Destitution   The Book of Syncopation   A Poet's Book of Rhythm two hands clapping two fingers tapping   The Book of Sacramental Visions   The Book of The Store a cross-dresser's handbook   The Red Book sold at street corners   The Addict's Book of Addiction   The Book of Excisions   A Chapbook of Genes or 'you can't help being'   The Book of Distortions latency is the book you hide behind The Book of Consolation   Book of Forensic Investigation subtitled the missing   The Book of Questions   Three Books on the Subject of Sin 'Guilt Self-Pity Hate'   The Best Book of Forgetting   The Book of Movement   A Small Book of Swallows   The Book of Dichotomies   a book of two halves Book of the Actual   Philosophy of the Whole Person subtitled finite being The Book of Agnostic Joy   Book of Exaltation   The Great Book is the God Question   A Small Book of Defiance   The Book of All We Don't Know Isn't Possible Ghost Book   The Big Book of War   God Illuminates subtitled the extra-ordinary   The Book of Persistent Sounds   Book of Primates Wo-Man

The Book of Ash In-spirited   The Book of Relations   A Book of Gifts my
mother gave me her gift of life   The Book of Human Dark   Round Book of
Moons   Six Books Bandaged in Skin The Book of Scars   The Book of Ash In-
spirited   Details Regarding the Mystery of Painting   The Book of the Image
not the Thing   The Book of Impure Language has no Name   Hymn to
Surrealist Art   The Wound Healing or the book of severed parts   A Woman's
Book of Bruises   The Refugee's Book of Power subtitled no loitering   The
Cold Book of Glaciers or the frozen heart the part you don't see   Particles a
book of minute matter   The Book of All we Consume   The Book of Clouds
The Magician's Book of the Real   Like a Victim a chapbook of shame   One
Book Too Many   Book of the Look   A Transparent Book to see through   The
Book of Erudition   The Book of the Twelve Tribes   Sand Songs for a Mother
A Book of Trace   hand print on a window   A Poet's Book of Hope
Compounded   The Book of Fear viral fever pseudo pains   The Book of All
you Meant to Say   The Book of Belief is Ancient   The Book of Loss is a Way
of Learning   Images of the Dead Mother   The Book of Fugitive Light also
called mysterious   The Death Book subtitled the divine.

# Place

I am near now  as it is happening
so close I can hear it echo
through the dark canal

I am not separate
I am not who I thought I was
I can still be naked
I can run into the forest
I can disable myself
I can be excluded from my own chaos
I can collapse dreams
into unmanageable flames

Standing beneath the archway
looking up at its perfect symmetry
I know    this is the place

My eyes smart: disseminate sharp light
Keep them open    Keep them wide open

# Acknowledgements

My thanks to the editors of the following publications in which some of these poems, or earlier versions of them, first appeared:

*The New Hibernian Review* USA (2014)

*Dream of a City Astrolabe Press* (2014)

*Stony Thursday* (2014, 2015, 2016 & 2018)

*Cyphers* 82 (2016)

*Washing Windows* (anthology, Arlen House, 2017)

*Even the Daybreak 35 Years of Salmon Poetry* (anthology, Salmon, 2016)

*Stinging Fly* (2017)

*Southword* (2017)

*Survision* 3 (2018) – www.survisionmagazine.com

*Cyphers* 86 (2018)

*The White Cottage Poems*. Limited edition chapbook publication T-A-R (2016)

Video on Vimeo: *The White Cottage Exhibition Jo Slade*. Spilt Milk Films UK (2016)

Heartfelt thanks to Jessie Lendennie & Siobhán Hutson at Salmon Poetry for their steadfast support over many years.

To those friends who gave close reading of the work and advice, I am deeply grateful. Special thanks to Fanny Howe.

Grateful thanks to The Arts Council of Ireland for a Literature Bursary in 2016 that supported this work.

# Notes

"Cycles and Lost Monkeys": The title for this poem was inspired by the painting, Hidden Men and Lost Monkeys, 2013, by Jules de Balincourt.

"Roll Along Covered Wagon": Song composed by the Irish song writer, Jimmy Kennedy in 1934.

"Palimpsest: An installation" by Doris Salcedo. Palacio de Cristal Madrid, 2018.

"Shelter": "Your sweet loving will make everything alright" from *Help Me Through the Day Help Me Through the Night*, a song written by Leon Russell & performed by Freddy King. Released 1973. "Gimme, gimme shelter," from *Gimme Shelter*, a song written & performed by the Rolling Stones. 1969.

"Compass: The Madres in the Plaza de Mayo," refers to the courageous mothers & grandmothers who have, for four decades, protested at the "disappearance" of their sons, husbands, brothers, lovers during the military dictatorship in Argentina 1976-83. Their 'white scarves' have become a symbol of courage. They continue their protest to this day.

"i.m. Tim": Dedicated to my brother, Tim Donnelly 1949 – 2014.

"The White Cottage": The installation/exhibition and the accompanying, limited edition chapbook, *The White Cottage* (T-A-R publications 2016) took place in The Sailor's Home, O'Curry Street, Limerick in November 2016.

The video on Vimeo: *The White Cottage* Exhibition Jo Slade (Spilt Milk Films, UK 2016).

*The White Cottage* or *The Little White House* is the name given to Bunker 2, (which was originally a woodsman's/farmer's cottage) at Auschwitz-Birkenau. Many women, children and men were murdered there in 1942, 1943, 1944. Edith Stein was murdered there and her sister Rosa on August 9th,1942. Edith Stein was a Jewish woman, a philosopher, a poet, a feminist, she became a Catholic, a Carmelite nun and was canonized in 1998. The installation/exhibition and chapbook were essentially a receptacle for the memory of Edith Stein's journey to her death. If the space of memory is fluid then the poems, the installation/exhibition & the video, The White Cottage, represent all genocides, those in the past and those taking place now, in our time. We are witness to this.

JO SLADE lives and works in Limerick. Poet and painter, she is the author of five collections of poetry and two chapbooks of poems, *The Artist's Room* (Pighog Press, Brighton, UK 2010), *The White Cottage* (T-A-R Publications 2016). Her most recent collection, *The Painter's House* (Salmon Poetry in 2013) was joint recipient of the Michael Hartnett Poetry Prize 2014. Other publications include: *In Fields I Hear Them Sing* (Salmon Publishing, 1989); *The Vigilant One* (Salmon Publishing 1994), nominated for The Irish Times/Aer Lingus Literature Prize; *Certain Octobers* (Editions Eireanna, Quimper, France, 1997) a dual language English/French edition, which received a publication bursary from the Centre du Livre, Paris, France; *City of Bridges* (Salmon Poetry, 2005), nominated in 2003 for the 'Prix Evelyn Encelot,' Ecriture Prize, Maison des Ecrivains, Paris. She has had poems translated into French, Spanish, Romanian, Norwegian, Russian, Italian & Slovenian, and poems published in literary journals and broadsheets in Northern Ireland, the UK, the USA, Canada, Russia, France, Slovenia, Spain, the Channel Islands & Italy. She was appointed as Writer-in-Residence for Limerick County Council in 2006 and writer-in-residence in the winter of 2007 at the Centre Culturel Irlandais, Paris, France. She is the recipient of a Literature Bursary & Travel Grants from The Arts Council of Ireland, Culture Ireland & Limerick City Council. She has exhibited her paintings widely in Ireland, France & Italy. Her most recent installation/exhibition took place in the Sailor's Home, Limerick, in 2016.

# salmonpoetry

Cliffs of Moher, County Clare, Ireland

"Like the sea-run Steelhead salmon that thrashes upstream to its spawning ground, then instead of dying, returns to the sea—Salmon Poetry Press brings precious cargo to both Ireland and America in the poetry it publishes, then carries that select work to its readership against incalculable odds."

TESS GALLAGHER

# The Salmon Bookshop & Literary Centre

Ennistymon, County Clare, Ireland

"Another wonderful Clare outlet."
*The Irish Times*, 35 Best Independent Bookshops